NO PLACE FOR A WOMAN
A PLAY WITH MUSIC AND MOVEMENT

By CORDELIA O'NEILL

Published by Playdead Press 2017

© Cordelia O'Neill 2017

Cordelia O'Neill has asserted her rights under the Copyright, Design and Patents Act, 1988, to be identified as the authors of this work.

A CIP catalogue record for this book is available from the British Library.

ISBN 978-1-910067-46-8

Caution
All rights whatsoever in this play are strictly reserved and application for performance should be sought through the author before rehearsals begin. No performance may be given unless a license has been obtained.

This book is sold subject to the condition that it shall not by way of trade or otherwise, be lent, resold, hired out, or otherwise circulated without the publisher's prior consent in any form of binding or cover other than that in which it is published and without a similar condition including this condition being imposed on the subsequent purchaser.

Playdead Press
www.playdeadpress.com

SMALL THINGS THEATRE in association with Theatre 503 present

NO PLACE FOR A WOMAN
A PLAY WITH MUSIC AND MOVEMENT
By **CORDELIA O'NEILL**

First performed at Theatre 503, Battersea, London on May 3rd 2017

NO PLACE FOR A WOMAN
A PLAY WITH MUSIC AND MOVEMENT
By **CORDELIA O'NEILL**

Annie **Ruth Gemmell**
Isabella **Emma Paetz**
Music/Cellist **Elliott Rennie**

Director **Kate Budgen**
Designer **Camilla Clarke**
Lighting **Sarah Readman**
Sound **Ella Wahlström**
Movement Director **Lucy Cullingford**
Production Manager **Rich Irvine**
Stage Manager **Rachel Darwood**
Producer **Philip Scott-Wallace**
Associate Producer **Audrey Thayer**
Dramaturg **Lauretta Barrow**

THE COMPANY

Ruth Gemmell | Annie

Theatre: *Midsummer Mischief, Midwinter, King Lear, Macbeth* (RSC), *Coram Boy* (National Theatre), *Sixty Six Books, Helter Skelter/Land of the Dead* (Bush Theatre), *Ancient Lights* (Hampstead Theatre) and *The Weir* (Royal Court)
TV: *Penny Dreadful* (Showtime/Sky) *Home Fires* (ITV) *Utopia* (C4).
Film: *Fever Pitch, Good.*

Emma Paetz | Isabella

Theatre: *You're Human Like the Rest of Them* (Finborough Theatre), *The Deep Blue Sea, Company, The Seagull, The Trojan Women* (in training at Guildhall School of Music and Drama)
Film: *Final Girl*

Elliott Rennie | Music and Cellist

As M.D and Composer: *The B.F.G* (Derby Theatre), *Fury* (Workshop: Soho Theatre), *Brainpeople* (Chaskis Theatre/Stratford East), *The Terrible Tale of the Twiddly Diddlies* (New Diorama), *Occupy, Slick, Skunk* and *Relish* (NYT). Theatre credits as actor include: *Shakespeare in Love* (Noel Coward Theatre), *Pinocchio* (Stephen Joseph Theatre), *The Trench* (Les Enfant Terribles International Tour), *Jekyll and Hyde* (Southwark Playhouse), *Faust* (Greenwich Theatre), *Sweet Charity* (MAC, Belfast).

Kate Budgen | Director

Kate trained at Birkbeck College and on the NT Studio Directors course. She was Associate Director at Pentabus Theatre from 2008-2011 and Creative Associate at the Bush Theatre from 2010-2011. Selected directing credits include: *Strong Arm* (Underbelly/Old Vic New Voices), *The Hairy Ape* (Southwark Playhouse) *Rigor Mortis* (Papatango /Finborough), *May Fair* (Pentabus Theatre), *Crossed Keys* (Eastern Angles), *Bedbound* (Lion and Unicorn), *Stoopud Fucken Animals* (Traverse Theatre), *There is a War* (Arts Ed) *Punk Rock* (Guildford School of Acting), *Anne Boleyn* (RWCMD). She has worked as Assistant Director for The Gate Theatre, The Almeida, The Opera Group, Pentabus Theatre, The Bush Theatre and for Opera North. She was Associate Director on *The Cripple of Inishmaan* for the Michael Grandage Company in 2013. She is a Connections Director for the National Theatre Connections Festival and has been a visiting director at Arts Educational Schools, the Actors Centre and LAMDA.

Cordelia O'Neill | Playwright

This is Cordelia's second full-length play. Her first, *The Stolen Inches* (Small Things Theatre), premiered at the Edinburgh Festival 2015 and was a sell-out receiving 4-star reviews. Other writing credits include *My ET* (Bites and Scratches at The Pleasance Islington), *Living in the City With or Without Sex* (The Old Red Lion Theatre). She trained as an actress at The Oxford School of Drama.

Camilla Clarke | Designer

Camilla is a Set & Costume designer based in London. She trained at the Royal Welsh College of Music and Drama, graduating in 2014 with First Class Honours in Theatre Design. In 2015 she was a winner of the Linbury Prize for Stage Design. Camilla was the recipient of the Prince of Wales Scholarship 2013, The Paul Klimpton prize for innovation in Design and The Lord Williams Memorial Prize for Design in 2014. Credits include: *Wind Resistance* (The Royal Lyceum Theatre, Edinburgh) and *Human Animals* (The Royal Court Theatre Upstairs).

Sarah Readman | Lighting Designer

Sarah is a multidisciplinary theatre practitioner working across theatre, circus and dance.
Recent credits include: *Hyena* (Jacksons Lane and London Wonderground), *This Beautiful Future* (Yard Theatre), *Fire In The Machine* (Battersea Arts Centre and The Albany Theatre), *Voodoo* (IBT International Showcase, LEAP Festival and Lillian Baylis Theatre, *The Foley Experiment* and *FCKSYSTMS* (Yard Theatre), *The Tempest, punkplay* and *Macbeth* (Southwark Playhouse), *This Place We Know* (Bush Theatre), *Fallow Cross* (Punchdrunk Enrichment)

Ella Wahlström | Sound Design

Ella is a London-based Sound Designer and trained at Rose Bruford. She was an original sound operator of Complicite's *The Encounter* a Co-Sound Designer of Robert Wilson and Mikhail Baryshnikov's *Letter to a*

Man and the Sound Designer of *Esa-Pekka Salonen's Cello Concerto*. Theatre Sound Design credits include: *Peter Pan Goes Wrong* (Mischief, West End), *Three Generations of Women* (Broken Leg Theatre Greenwich Theatre), *The Life* (English Theatre Frankfurt), *The Ballad of Robin Hood* (Tacit Theatre, Southwark Playhouse), *The Bunker Trilogy, The Frontier Trilogy and The Capone Trilogy* (Jethro Compton, Edinburgh Fringe and international touring), *Empty Vessels* (Rosemary Branch Theatre), *Sirenia* (Jethro Compton, Edinburgh Fringe), *Klippies* (Southwark Playhouse), *Chicken Dust* (Finborough Theatre), *In Lambeth* (Spellbound Productions, Southwark Playhouse), *Carroll: Berserk* (Spindrift Theatre, Drayton Arms Theatre), *A Study in Scarlet* (Tacit Theatre, Southwark Playhouse), *Titus Andronicus* (Hiraeth, Arcola), *Romeo and Juliet* (Hiraeth, Upstairs at the Gatehouse), *Theatre Uncut* (Theatre Uncut, Young Vic), *The Revenger's Tragedy and Henry V* (Old Red Lion Theatre). As Associate Sound Designer: *Othello* (Frantic Assembly), *JOHN* (DV8), *The Cripple of Inishmaan* (Michael Grandage Company).

Lucy Cullingford | Movement Director

Lucy was movement practitioner in the Movement Department of The Royal Shakespeare Company for two years and is currently Movement Director for *The Tempest* (RSC). Previous collaborations include *Don Quixote, The Jew of Malta*, David Farr's *The Winter's Tale*, Greg Doran's *Hamlet, Loves Labors Lost* and *A Midsummer Night's Dream* (Courtyard Theatre). Lucy is currently Dance Repetiteur for the RSC's production of *Matilda The Musical*.

Rich Irvine | Production Manager

Recent Theatrical Production Manager credits include: *This Beautiful Future* (Yard Theatre), *Lottery of Love* (Orange Tree Theatre), *BU21* (Trafalgar Studious), *Scrooge And Seven Dwarves* (Theatre 503), *Carry On Jaywick* (Touring), *PunkPlay* (Southwark Playhouse), *Screens* (Theatre 503)
Deputy Technical Manager: *Vaults Festival 2017*.

Rachel Darwood | Stage Manager

Since graduating from Rose Bruford College of Theatre and Performance in 2014, Rachel has worked on a variety of productions including tours, operas, open-air, musicals, and plays. Her most recent productions include, *The Book's the Thing* and *A Christmas Carol* with Librarian Theatre, *Phone Home*, an international production with Munich and Athens regarding the refugee crisis, at Shoreditch Town Hall and *The Funfair* at the Academy of Live and Recorded Arts (ALRA). When not working as a Stage Manager, Rachel works as a member of the technical crew with ESS Hire – most recently working on the Jack Petchey Glee Club Challenge. Every year Rachel enjoys going back to the Twinwood Vintage Festival where she works as one of the stage managers.

Philip Scott-Wallace | Producer

Philip is a founding director of Small Things Theatre. Producing credits include: *The Stolen Inches* (Edinburgh

Festival 2015), *Night of Small Things* (regular variety night at The Old Red Lion Theatre) and *A Gym Thing* (Pleasance Courtyard, Edinburgh Festival 2017), which he will also direct. He trained as an actor at LAMDA and credits include: *Alligators* (Hampstead Theatre), *Bash* (Trafalgar Studios), *Downton Abbey* (ITV).

Audrey Thayer | Associate Producer

Programming Director of Drayton Arms Theatre and Freelance Producer as well as a writer, dramaturg, and theatre maker. *Rapid Write Response, Top Trumps* (Resident Assistant Producer, Theatre 503). *You're Human Like the Rest of Them* (Producer, Finborough Theatre).

The Small Things Theatre Company was formed in 2015 by Philip Scott-Wallace and Cordelia O'Neill. We aspire to delight, fascinate and challenge by producing new theatre from emerging artists. Our first production was *The Stolen Inches* by Cordelia O'Neill, which achieved a sell-out run at Edinburgh Fringe Festival 2015. Alongside our plays we collaborate with, help nurture and provide a platform for playwrights, actors, musicians, comedians and poets through our regular *Night Of Small Things* at The Old Red Lion Theatre. *No Place For A Woman* began life as a fifteen-minute excerpt at *A Night Of Small Things* before being developed into a full-length play.

We also have a thriving education department providing bespoke Shakespeare workshops, inspiring students of all ages to engage with drama.

Theatre allows us to see things from other people's perspective and Small Things Theatre believe it is a force for good that can help, heal, unite as well as thoroughly entertain.

So why Small Things? As well as our mission statement above we delight in the small moments in drama that move hearts and minds. A look, a sigh, a move or a single word can make your heart burst or your gut drop and it is only the most exquisite productions that find these minute details to bring the stage alive. It is our desire to produce all our work with moments that reflect how wonderfully nuanced life is, reminding our audiences that it is often the small things that make a big difference.

Small Things Theatre would like to thank the entire cast and creative team, all those at Theatre 503 especially Lisa Spirling and Andrew Shepherd as well as the following people, all of whom have contributed to the play:

Georgina Fairbanks
Harriet Olins
Sarah Longson
Julianna Bautista
Caroline Faber
Kirsten Obank
Andrew Burton
Anthony Lee

And for their endless support, we thank:
Rory and Pepi O'Neill
George and Val Wallace

www.smallthingstheatre.com

Twitter: @smallthingstc

Instagram: @smallthingstheatre

Facebook: /smallthingstheatre

Praise for SMALL THINGS THEATRE'S *The Stolen Inches* by Cordelia O'Neill

'subversive and intriguing piece of social satire'

– The Scotsman

'Cordelia O'Neill's cleverly constructed play (has) pager-turner tension'

– The Stage

'The Small Things Theatre Company presents a touching and often hilarious examination of a family struggling to keep up appearances... a must see domestic drama, beautifully put together'

– A Younger Theatre

Supported by

The Drop

Drop is a delivery service that brings top quality, expertly chosen, great value wines to your doorstep, workplace or picnic rug without the hassle of a minimum spend or delivery charge.

To download the app visit www.dropwine.co.uk

Theatre503 is a 60-seat new writing powerhouse situated in the heart of Battersea, South London. It launches the work of more new writers than any other theatre in the UK and is the smallest theatre in the world to have won an Olivier award (for Katori Hall's *The Mountaintop*). Playwrights whose careers started at the theatre include Tom Morton Smith (*Oppenheimer*), Anna Jordan (*Yen*), Dennis Kelly (*Matilda the Musical*) and Katori Hall (*Photograph 51*).

Artistic Director	Lisa Spirling
Executive Director	Andrew Shepherd
Producer	Jessica Campbell
Literary Manager	Steve Harper
Literary Coordinators	Lauretta Barrow, Wayne Brown
Operations Manager	Anna DeFreitas
Marketing Coordinator	Rebecca Usher
Technical Manager	Alastair Borland
Resident Assistant Producers	Michelle McKay, Pippa Davis

OUR BOARD OF TRUSTEES

Erica Whyman (Chair)	Deputy Artistic Director, Royal Shakespeare Company
Royce Bell (Vice Chair)	Chair, Punchdrunk Theatre
Chris Campbell	Literary Manager, Royal Court Theatre
Kay Ellen Consolver	Independent Board Director, Multiple Organisations
Joachim Fleury	Partner, Clifford Chance
Celine Gagnon	Chief Executive, The Funding Network

Eleanor Lloyd	Producer, Eleanor Lloyd Productions
Marcus Markou	Filmmaker, Entrepreneur
Geraldine Sharpe-Newton	Communications Strategist
Jack Tilbury	Director, Plann Ltd
Roy Williams OBE	Playwright

Theatre503 would not be successful without the amazing support we receive from our dedicated team of volunteers:
Kelly Agredo, Rosie Akerman, Serafina Cusack, Mark Doherty, Bridget Rudder, Darren Siah, Rob Ellis, Tom Hartwell, George Linfield, Mike Murgaz, Mandy Nicholls, Annabel Pemberton, Andrei Vornicu, Emily Standring, Simon Mander, Mike McGarry, Phoebe Hyder, Nicole Zweiback, Suzanne Brewis, Nathalie Czarnecki, Emma Griffiths, Asha Osborne, Carla Kingham, Emma Griffiths and Aydan Tair

OUR SUPPORTERS
We are incredibly grateful to the following who have supported us recently without whom our work would not be possible:
The Harold Hyman Wingate Foundation, The Schroder Charity Trust, The Boris Karloff Foundation, The Idelwild Trust, Cockayne Grants for the Arts, The Peter Wolff Trust, The Sylvia Waddilove Foundation, The Thistle Trust, The Unity Theatre Trust, The Williams Trust, The Audience Club, M&G Investments, Barbara Broccoli, Wandsworth Council, Arts Council England Grants for the Arts, all our Friends, Patrons and Point of Sale Donors.

We are currently in receipt of funding from Arts Council England's Catalyst Evolve fund – allowing us to grow our fundraising capacity by match funding income from new donors over the next three years. Particular thanks to the Richard Carne Trust for their generous support of our Playwriting Award and 503 Five.

A note on the play
The play is set in Poland 1945 at the end of World War Two. Two women are being interviewed by the Allied forces.

Characters

Isabella

Annie

Musician

Scene 1

ISABELLA:

Do you mind if I take off my coat?

It's fine

I don't think I'll feel cold anymore

She takes off the coat

No

Pause

Not one chill

I'd been waiting

In that room

For what felt like forever

And now you're here it's over.

I don't mind waiting

Don't think it's torture for me

Waiting is one of the safest things you can do.

Don't you think?

Waiting for something to happen.

In that time, in that place, it's the same, it's all as you once knew it.

I'd like to sit and wait a little longer

But I can't

You won't let me

And now

Is she here?

Did you find her?

ANNIE:

Sat silently smoking, She suddenly shivers

It's cold?

Do you think it's cold or is it just me?

I know it's spring but...

The windows are locked up so it can't be them.

Is there a gap in the door?

I expect there is a gap in the door, it's probably not fitted correctly

Nothing has ever fitted in this house

We've had constant issues

That must be what it is.

The gap, in the door.

There must be a draft.

You'll want to speak to someone about that.

I lost my coat

Did you know that

I lost my darling coat

It just vanished

Don't mention it

Please

It was a present you see

And

It'll be terribly upsetting

Should…

Yes I think it is the door

You must get it fixed.

It's far too cold in here.

ISABELLA:

You fixed the door

I noticed the light

From the corridor yesterday

A big bolt of light that cast half your face in shadow

But now I can see you

Every bit of you

And you can see me

Where do you come from?

Do you miss it?

Will you go back to the same place?

The same people

The same life

Of course you will.

ANNIE:

Your cigarette keeps going out

What's the point of having it if you keep letting it go out?

I hate this room

How dare you bring me here.

ISABELLA:

You can't rush me

You have to listen

And it may take some time.

But it's my turn now

To make people wait

So be patient

And understand

You must try to understand

Scene 2

ISABELLA:	**ANNIE:**
	It's funny what you remember
First position	
	What events stick in your mind
Second position	There was no Champagne
Third, fourth and fifth	Not a drop

ISABELLA:

Now for the arms,

First, second, third, fourth, fifth

Then we have a plié, releve and sauté.

Excellent work, excellent work, look at you.

Now first position feet, fourth position hands plié, releve, sauté

They put me with the children when I arrived. I don't think they were sure where to place me, Aus, Aus, Aus they screamed as the train pulled up, there was no time to say goodbye.

I suppose it was the ballet dancers body. My sister Margo says it's a curse and I always thought it was, flat as a pancake and no hips, dress me in a shorts and jacket and I'm a boy, without question.

Margo has a woman's figure Mama says a figure made for bearing, bearing cakes and strudels more like. Every Sunday on the way to class Margo would stop at Madam Schinifers shop and buy an apple and cinnamon strudel.

They were huge, they were delicious, they were heaven.

They were not for ballet dancers.

We would arrive and warm up with spotting, find a spot in the room place your feet, hold and spin and spin and spin and spin

Without question fifteen minutes in Margo would be sick, she would vomit her breakfast of heaven and have to sit out of class.

Five weeks she did this sneaky trick, until Mama was brought into school and told that maybe her daughter should look into a career as a baker not a dancer.

And still she eats the strudel every Sunday.

Shhhhh shhhh children, ballet dancers are always silent, music is their voice and their body is their language. Don't speak children. Please don't speak.

Shall we go again?

First and second and third and fourth and fifth.

I was praised for my "perfect dancing hands", Mademoiselle Foley said. I do have nice hands I think. Mama for my birthday bought me some cream from Paris especially for your hands it was Chanel, every night I would drop the tiniest amount and rub every bit of my hand even my lines, especially my life line, Mama says I have a long life line. See

And that I must always take care it does not shrink, so I must eat all my greens and drink water and not eat strudel like Margo.

Margo has the deepest longest lifeline, it looks like someone sliced her hand open, she never eats her greens and her hand says she'll live the longest.

I hope she does live the longest.

ANNIE:

Last summer I threw a garden party, there were always parties in Berlin. We had Champagne then, but there was this silly waitress who was serving the Champagne to the guests as they arrived.

All she had to do was stand still with a tray in her hand, like this

She shows the interviewer what she means

I left her for half an hour and then I turn round and see her arm just drop and all the Champagne glasses smash. That was ten glasses gone.

She didn't have a straight spine, I should have known, she couldn't have been much younger than me and still serving Champagne.

I had the straightest spine, I could walk around the room for hours with a book on my head, we had a competition once between me and another girl in school; Elise, was her name.

We both stood still while the other girls placed one book after another on top. Ten books made me the winner.

That's the only thing I've ever won

So they tell us that there will be no Champagne, I can't talk to Fredrick, you understand. I can't talk to him about this. Maybe we could serve a short drink to begin with, not a Champagne. Will that be alright do you think?

Fredrick and I met at the ballet, in Berlin. I was only 18 and I was crying when he met me, imagine that. I was looking a fright and I met Fredrick.

He asked me if I found the ballet as boring as he did, and was that why I was crying.

I laughed and told him the opposite that I love the ballet so much it made me weep.

With my spine I should have been a dancer that's what they all say

But

Why dance around a stage when you can dance around a room imagine what people would say if they saw Captain

Annhult's daughter wearing her underwear in front of everyone.

I suppose I understand.

So Fredrick met me crying over the Ballet and we fell in love.

Sometimes I have days when I'm not myself and Fredrick is the only person who can make me better, he tells me to remember when I was crying at the ballet and that soon I stopped crying.

"Remember that," he says, "remember that feeling of stopping."

"Yes," I say.

"Good my love, now stop."

And I do, just like that because of my sweet Fredrick.

So we will definitely not have Champagne at the party, that will be fine I'm sure, don't you think?

No one will mind too much.

ISABELLA:

Are you cold? You shouldn't be, it's spring.

At ballet school it was always cold so me and the girls would leap from the corner to stay warm. When the heating went I made my family do the same, Papa, Mama, Margo, Jack.

They were so funny, Margo with her clumsy limbs nearly knocked over a vase Mama and Papa got for their wedding. The whole room went silent then Papa picked it up and smashed the vase against the wall.

Just like that

When he turned around he was crying

ANNIE:

Our house in Berlin was so beautiful.

I miss it

We had so many rooms that when we first had Jennifer if she cried we never heard her.

I never heard her anyway

When she was born I was ill again and I didn't have the energy, I didn't have the energy to hear her, I didn't have the energy to feed her. I just sat and looked at our beautiful house.

ISABELLA:

Beautiful children you are so good.

This is cold this place, and I'm not sure even dancing can warm us up.

ANNIE:

This is different this house, I have no doubt it's beautiful but it's different.

Great things are happening

Right now this minute our world is changing and this house is part of that change.

I never see Fredrick anymore.

I'm not allowed to visit him, it's just not appropriate. And I have important work here in the house, the staff, the children, who will watch the children?

I think they hate me, the children, I really think they do hate me.

I told Fredrick this and he laughed.

How can a child hate anyone, especially their mother, children are innocent.

I don't know I said, anyway I don't need them I have you.

But I don't have him at the moment, not with the new job and all the new responsibility.

It's such a privilege to be asked, I think. That's why we are having the party to say thank you for everything, the job the house the new car.

I just don't think the party will be the same without Champagne.

It'll be terribly upsetting if everything isn't perfect, if it's not how it's meant to be, if I fail.

They must have some at the offices.

They're always raising a toast to something, someone.

Fredrick's so busy I'm sure he'll forget if I ask him

He would understand,

It's for the party, for him.

It'll only take a second. I promise

No one will even see me.

It'll be our secret

Go on then

Go on

Call the driver.

We'll need the car.

ISABELLA:

Children, you all need to take off your clothes

Stop it, stop crying

Put on the costumes they have given us

Yes costumes.

This is what you will wear in the performance. We're going outside, to show everyone your beautiful costumes. Maybe your families will see.

That's why you're here, to practice and learn for your performance.

Now first positions.

Oh well done, and remember shhhhhhhh just be quiet.

ANNIE:

Is that?

Is that my coat

You found it

You have found my coat

Do you like it?

It was a wedding present from Fredrick's mother.

She strokes the coat

I love it so much

He won't mind

He will want me looking my best

In front of all the officers.

And of course we have to have Champagne

Is this really my coat?

She hugs the coat around her and starts to sway on the spot, gently humming a tune.

ISABELLA:

And 1, 2, 3, 4, 1, 2, 3, 4, 1, 2, 3, 4

And open,

Forward plié

Down and up and stretch

Little forward bend

And up

Lift again

Demi Plié

And arms and arms and arms

She repeats then slowly she forgets where she is and who she is teaching and just starts dancing.

Annie begins to sway at the same time as Isabella's counting, Isabella teaches the children a routine. The further into the routine we get, Annie's humming slowly melts into music and she begins to dance the same steps that Isabella is telling the children. Isabella can't resist but embrace the routine she is teaching and slowly and surely Isabella and Annie are dancing the same dance at the same time.

They both pivot at the same time and turn to face one another and stop dancing, they look at each other, through each other.

Scene 3

ISABELLA:

They found me out

I'm not a child

I'm a woman.

"You're no child," he said

"Children are innocent and innocence can't dance like you can."

ANNIE:

They were all lined up

Three groups

Men

Women

Children

An officer drove me up to the gates and told me to wait, that it was no place for a woman.

"What's your name?"

"Karl Daschner"

"That's my husband"

"Will you keep me from him?"

"I'm under orders", (he said)

"Karl Daschner. I'll be sure to repeat that name carefully when my husband next makes his recommendations for the front line"

I heard Fredrick's voice and followed it

ISABELLA: Who can play?

ANNIE: They were all lined up.

ISABELLA: He wanted to know if there were any musicians

ANNIE: Who can play?

ISABELLA: No one moved

"Who can play?"

He said again

Still no one moved

"WHO CAN PLAY"

Even if you wanted to move you couldn't

He went silent and walked around us, he pulled a man out of a line

Brought him in front of us

Asked one more time

"Who can play?"

Not an inch no one moved an inch

So he shot him

In the head

And asked again

"Who can play?"

I can dance I whispered

ANNIE:

He was holding an audition

For the party

For my party

He was finding me musicians

I wanted a band from Berlin to come and play but because of the snow they'd never make it

So Fredrick was finding a band for me.

He's so good

And they ignored him, they ignored his opportunity.

How rude

How rude not to want to come to our house and play, to play music to make people dance

How rude to ignore my Fredrick.

ISABELLA:

He was old

His back stooped slightly. But he played beautifully

And he liked him, he was silent and just watched the old man play.

He was crying. I was crying and he was crying. We were both crying at the same thing.

I hated myself. One of his officers coughed and he kicked him.

We were there for hours

He made the old man play for hours

ANNIE:

It was so wonderful

Such brilliant music

How lucky we all were to stand and listen to our own concert, if I closed my eyes I felt like I was at the ballet. I do so love the ballet. Fredrick did this for me, he knew I'd come, and he wanted to surprise me. How kind he is. To give me this gift and to let them all listen and watch with me.

ISABELLA:

He was getting tired

I could tell

The beats were longer, the music was slower

If he stops, if that old man stops before he says so, he's dead.

1 and 2 and 3 and 4

And 1 and 2 and 3 and 4

And 1 and 2 and 3 and 4

ANNIE:

She was beautiful

He watched her

He watched her dance in the snow

"I don't remember asking for dancers, I specifically said musicians Fredrick, just a little group in the corner so we don't have to see them. I don't remember asking for dancers."

"Do you remember?" he said

"When I first met you,"

"And you were crying,"

"Yes"

"Well stop crying and go to bed."

ISABELLA:

He stood when I started

I knew the steps, it wasn't hard

My boots were too big for me so they slipped off easily

The snow stung at first but soon I forgot and

I just danced

He stopped me, grabbed my hands and held me in front of him

"If I die I don't care, at least I got to dance," I thought. But I didn't die. He lifted his hand as if he was going to hit me and then placed it on my cheek, like Papa used to.

ANNIE:

He should have shot her

I've seen him do it with birds

Doesn't even look

Just points and shoots

ISABELLA:

I could have been shot

ANNIE:

He hates ballet

ISABELLA:

Instead I was to dance at a party

ANNIE:

She's to dance at my party

Scene 4

ANNIE: Are you ready?

ISABELLA: Can you imagine?

ANNIE: Your shoes have been polished, I made sure to have your shoes polished before tonight.

ISABELLA: Being here

ANNIE: They're fine

ISABELLA: No, you can't

ANNIE: They're fine

ISABELLA: Can you?

ANNIE: Fredrick, I said they're fine

ISABELLA: Can you?

Pause

ISABELLA: Do you know I had nowhere to… do it

There was nowhere discreet

No cup

No bowl

No.

Nowhere

So I just stood

Just stood

Stood there and…

ANNIE: It's half past six

People are arriving at eight o'clock

And when they arrive

Where will you be?

Where will you be?

ISABELLA: The warmth

Was so

Lovely

And do you know what

I thought of my family

She starts to laugh

As I stood there

And that warm sensation trickled down my legs

I started to think of my family

ANNIE: Stop saying that

Stop saying you have to go

You don't

You don't have to go anywhere

My hair isn't the same is it?

It's just not quite right

ISABELLA: I could smell perfume

ANNIE: Can you see Fredrick?

ISABELLA: It was seeping in from the other room

ANNIE: It doesn't twist in the same way does it?

ISABELLA: Through the gap in the door

ANNIE: Not like it used to

ISABELLA: Strong wafts of the stuff

ANNIE: Shall I just leave it

ISABELLA: I dare you

ANNIE: And maybe have it down

ISABELLA: To think of it

ANNIE: Fredrick?

ISABELLA: Think of the smell

ANNIE: It's a bit different isn't it

ISABELLA: The smell of those women.

ANNIE: Not appropriate

ISABELLA: Why?

ANNIE: It gives the wrong impression

ISABELLA: I don't care

ANNIE: I always used to have it like this didn't I

ISABELLA: Do it.

ANNIE: Like this

ISABELLA: No?

ANNIE: Fredrick?

ISABELLA: You wont even imagine

ANNIE: I was quite pretty back then.

ISABELLA: Yes?

ANNIE: No, it isn't quite right.

ISABELLA: No.

ANNIE: Up it goes

ISABELLA: You don't *want* to imagine

ANNIE: Yes.

ISABELLA: You never will

ANNIE: Perfect

ISABELLA: Because you're scared

ANNIE: Why are you leaving?

ISABELLA: You're scared

ANNIE: You're making me feel

ISABELLA: *(laughing)* Scared of only smelling

ANNIE: You're making me feel rushed

ISABELLA: Those women

ANNIE: I need you…

ISABELLA: Scared of imagining what they looked like

ANNIE: To help me finish

ISABELLA: Because then you have to picture me

Alone in this room

Covered in…

Waiting to

Dance

For the women

Whose perfume seeped through the walls

And the man

Who…

ANNIE: Will you just stop Fred, for a moment.

Pause

ISABELLA: What were their dresses like do you think?

ANNIE: See, my dress isn't

ISABELLA: Detailed

ANNIE: Look, It's quite fiddly

ISABELLA: Colourful

ANNIE: Do you remember this dress

ISABELLA: Clean

ANNIE: That night

ISABELLA: Not like mine

ANNIE: Years ago

Pause

ANNIE: A moment more Fredrick

ISABELLA: He saw, that I

ANNIE: You always button up the back of my dress

ISABELLA: He came in

ANNIE: You're trying to leave again…

ISABELLA: And said nothing

ANNIE: Come back

ISABELLA: 1 and 2 and 3 and 4

ANNIE: Fredrick

ISABELLA: I did it

ANNIE: My dress

ISABELLA: I danced

ANNIE: You always button up the back of my dress

ISABELLA: I danced

Brilliantly

I think

In the middle of the clouds of perfume

And the smell made me believe I was somewhere else

When I danced I was alone when I danced I was safe when I danced I could finally breathe.

But

Every moment my feet left the ground I wanted to keep going up and up and up

Every time I stretched my arm or pointed my toe I wanted to keep on going until my body split

Not in half but apart

I wanted my limbs to scatter all over the floor

I wanted my bones to break

And my fall to be hard

And I wanted to never dance again

In that moment

In the clouds of perfume

Covered in piss

But I did

I did dance

Brilliantly

I think

ANNIE: I do so love the ballet.

I whispered in his ear

Fredrick

He didn't hear me

I suppose the music was too loud

He probably couldn't hear himself think

Fredrick

He slowly turned around

Looked at me and said

Nothing

Nothing

And then it was over

And she was taken away.

ISABELLA:

Into this room

This very room.

Scene 5

Isabella begins her dance of assault while Annie narrates her first dance with Fred.

ANNIE: I could have been a dancer did you know that

1 and 2 and 3 and 4 and 1 and 2 and 3 and 4

We danced on our wedding day

Have you seen?

There were photographs

Over there

On the desk

Can you?

That's Fredrick and I, dancing

I dragged him up

The music started, I rested my cheek on his chest, I closed my eyes and we danced

1,2,3 1,2,3, 1,2,3, 1,2,3

His hand, tightly around my waist

Never let go

I promise

He spun me slowly out

Brought me back to him

Tucked my hair behind my ear

And stroked the side of my face

And even though everyone was watching

He kissed me

Very slowly

Down the side of my neck

Then we just gently rocked back and forth back and forth

Sometimes

When I'm on my own

I pretend

I place my hand on his shoulder

I feel his arm around my waist

And rest my face gently on his chest

And I imagine

Fredrick and I are back there

At our wedding

I can feel the kisses even now

I can feel them

On my neck

123, 123, 123, 123,

Rocking back and forth back and forth

With my darling Fredrick

He asked me

And I simply told him

Where to go

Where he could find her

He was so fat

I remember thinking, there's so much of you, you're sure to

Crush her

I sent him here

The fat man

The man who wanted to ...

Isabella's dance ends at this point

ISABELLA:

I could feel it, the calmness, the stillness.

That's how everything begins doesn't it with a calmness

Just before...

1, 2, 3, 4

I saw my family, laughing and dancing in the living room to warm up.

Then, just my Mama, standing in the doorway watching

It's alright Mama, I'm fine I said to her. I'm looking after my lifeline.

Then everything stopped and he fell on top of me

The sweat from his forehead dripped onto my face

The man was kicked off me

And he was there

He picked me up and put me on the sofa.

"Stop crying," he said

"Stop crying"

"Remember that feeling"

"Remember that feeling of stopping"

ANNIE:

I watched from the door.

The whole thing

Her nose was bleeding

And when Fredrick picked her up

He wiped it away with his sleeve

All I could see was her blood slowly seeping into his shirt

She was so small.

It was like watching a little dance.

ISABELLA: I'd like to leave

ANNIE: Why?

ISABELLA: Because

ANNIE: Now is not the time

ISABELLA: Do you want me to...

ANNIE: What?

ANNIE: No, Not like that

ISABELLA: I'm sorry

ANNIE: Never like that

ISABELLA: That's why I'm here?

ANNIE: It's not.

ISABELLA: Can I leave?

ANNIE: Why would you leave, where would you go?

ISABELLA: To where you found me

ANNIE: Why would you go back there?

ISABELLA: Why would you keep me here

ANNIE: Because I saw you

ISABELLA: Saw me what?

Pause

ANNIE: I saw you looking tired tonight my love

ISABELLA: I'm fine

ANNIE: You need looking after

ISABELLA: I need

ANNIE: Your love, your Annie

ISABELLA: My family

ANNIE: Wasn't it lovely to hear the music, how long has it been since you heard such good music

ISABELLA: Years

ANNIE: Well, there you go, what a thing to hear it again.

ISABELLA: Are they safe?

ANNIE: Forget them.

ISABELLA: People were shot, when I left

ANNIE: Let's not do this Fredrick.

ISABELLA: People were lined up and shot

ANNIE: I'm sorry

ISABELLA: Were my family shot?

ANNIE: I know how you must feel.

ISABELLA: How do you know?

ANNIE: Because I'm your

ISABELLA: You're my what?

ANNIE: Wife

ISABELLA:

ANNIE: So I must know, don't you think?

Pause

ISABELLA: How do you know they weren't

ANNIE: I just do

ISABELLA: I'd like to leave

ANNIE: People will talk they are already talking.

ISABELLA: Then let me go

ANNIE: I can't

ISABELLA: I danced

ANNIE: I want you to stay.

ISABELLA: Why?

ANNIE: Because

ISABELLA: I can't be here

ANNIE: Why?

ISABELLA: Were they shot.

ANNIE: You will stop talking about it. I can't bear to hear you talk about it anymore.

ISABELLA: When we were rounded up a woman stole my luggage. She was like a shadow running up and down the lines of families on the streets. Jumping on people, stealing their coats, hats, their food parcels, anything she could carry. She took Mama's, then mine and then she tried to take Papa's. But he resisted and said "Don't just take, ask my dear." She stopped and looked at him. Her eyes were hollow, her skin was grey and she had hair growing from her chin. I couldn't look at her. But Papa held her gaze and said.

"Now child, what can I do for you?"

"My baby, I need to feed my baby"

"Here"

And he handed her some bread from his suitcase. She snatched it off him and then pulled some bloody rags out of her pocket. She started feeding the bread to the rags.

"Hush hush" she whispered

And we watched as the bread crumbled to the floor.

ANNIE:

He didn't make love to me that night, he didn't come and find me.

I dressed in my finest outfit the following morning, a peacock blue dress with a purple hem, the sleeves long with a Sabrina neckline, and down the back it was fastened with gold buttons. I wore my pearls and had Hanna pin my hair. I still had some rouge so applied the smallest amount to my lips and cheeks. The trick, I've learnt, is to apply then rub it off, then re-apply and rub it off again. It gives the impression of very little effort.

She was to stay in the cellar that is what we agreed that is what we decided that is how it was to work.

Scene 6

ISABELLA:

Nothing happened for a very long time.

Then he came in

ANNIE: Fredrick wasn't at breakfast, so he didn't see my dress.

ISABELLA: He didn't speak

ANNIE: He wasn't at lunch

ISABELLA: He didn't look at me

ANNIE: He hasn't come back from work yet, has he?

ISABELLA: He just sat and stared

ANNIE: Will you tell him, if you see him, that I'm here.

ISABELLA: One morning

I woke

And on the floor

I remember a vase

With a flower in it.

ANNIE: Did he get it? Do you know? I left it for him, just one, it shows spring is coming. He'd like that, to be reminded.

ISABELLA: The next day

He brought a book.

Looked straight at me.

And started to quietly count 1, 2, 3, 4, 5, 6, 7, 8, 9, 10, 11, 12

ANNIE:

I tend to forget I have children

Do you know that?

Of course you do.

For just a second

I tend to forget

I need constant reminding

Dear little things

He sent them away when she arrived, far far away.

"Go kiss your Mother goodbye"

I bent my check towards their faces and they placed their last kisses here and here.

And then we were alone

The three of us

ISABELLA:

When he finished counting

He sat on the floor of the cellar and asked me to hold his hand

And I refused.

When he left me

Finally

I got up

And danced

For my family.

ANNIE:

I heard things

Things smashing and

Well this is his room no one is allowed in here

So

You're thinking "Did she really just stand at the door and listen"

Yes I did

I stood by the door

"Stop"

"Stop"

"Stop"

"Please my Darling stop"

Then he did just like that

But

He opened the door and saw me

I should have run away

Like a little rat.

Why didn't I run away?

There was sweat all over his face

He was so red

He stormed at me, grabbed my shoulders and shoved me in the room. There were papers, and maps and documents everywhere he piled as much as he could in my arms, and told me to throw them in the fire. But there was too much, there was just too much for me to carry, so I dropped them. He got my hands and forced them to grip the papers, then he pushed me towards the fire, pulled my arms apart and everything floated into the flames

ISABELLA: You never told me

How she was?

ANNIE: Do I look old?

I feel it.

ISABELLA: When you found her.

ANNIE: You won't even look at me

ISABELLA: I'm sorry

ANNIE: Even an apology is to the floor

ISABELLA: How would you like me to look at you?

ANNIE: Like you love me

ISABELLA: I do

ANNIE: Do I disgust you?

ISABELLA: No

ANNIE: If you loved me you would look at me,

ISABELLA: I am looking at you

ANNIE: You would long to look at me, you won't even be near me.

ISABELLA: I'm here.

ANNIE: So am I

ISABELLA: What do you want me to do?

ANNIE: To be my husband

ISABELLA: To care for you

ANNIE: Yes

ISABELLA: To hold you

ANNIE: Yes

ISABELLA: No

ANNIE: Why

ISABELLA: Because...

ANNIE: Have I hurt you

ISABELLA: No

ANNIE: Have I offended you?

ISABELLA: No

ANNIE: Then love me.

ISABELLA: How do you want me to love you?

ANNIE: What kind of a question is that?

ISABELLA: I don't understand; I don't know how to love you.

ANNIE: As I love you.

ISABELLA: Is that all you need, my love? Why my love? Why not your wife's or your children's? Why me?

ANNIE: They're nothing.

ISABELLA: They are your family?

ANNIE: Just sit beside me please

ISABELLA: I can't

ANNIE: Please

Pause

ANNIE: You're my...

ISABELLA: What?

ANNIE: Fredrick

ISABELLA: I'm not

Pause

ANNIE: They hate me, I told you the children hate me

ISABELLA: And if I love you, you will be better

ANNIE: Sometimes I am not myself

ISABELLA: If I love you all will be well

ANNIE: You are the only one that can make me better

ISABELLA: I hate you

I hate you

ANNIE: Stop

ISABELLA: I hate the smell of you

ANNIE: Stop it

ISABELLA: I hate the feel of you

ANNIE: Why are you being so cruel

ISABELLA: I hear screams

ANNIE: Kiss me

ISABELLA: I always hear screams

ANNIE: Lie with me

ISABELLA: Do you? Do you ever hear the people you killed. My people.

ANNIE: Lie with me.

ISABELLA: Lie with the ones that are dead,

Kiss them. Kiss their faces.

Cover yourself with the smell of the people you murdered

The men, the women, the children

Who no longer live because of you

You're disgusting

I am alone

I am so alone

You ask me to love you?

You tell me that all you need is my love

How can I love, how can I love anything anymore?

Annie goes to touch Fred and Isabella flinches

ANNIE: Please Fredrick

ISABELLA: The water tastes of shit

You keep filling up your glass

But the water tastes of shit

I won't drink it

Do you know where it comes from

The river

It's filtered from the river

You know what they put in the river don't you

That's why it tastes of shit

You shouldn't drink it

ANNIE:

Fredrick's family have farms near Munich. When we first married we went riding. I told him I had never been before, horse riding,

"Not even sat on a horse," I said.

So imagine his surprise when I galloped off into the distance. We spent all day away from the house and made love in the fields. I looked deep into his eyes and said to him, "This is it isn't it? This is Love"

His Mother sent out a search party, that's how long we were gone. They found us.

They say horses are a good judge of character. Did you know that? I would like a horse. I would like to ride a horse and disappear with Fredrick.

Scene 7

ISABELLA:

It was strange hearing their names again

For the first time

Since

From his mouth

They didn't feel like mine

When he said their names out loud to me

In his accent

They didn't feel like mine

Albert Weiss

Sara Weiss

Margo Weiss

Jack Weiss

That's them

That's my family

ANNIE:

Fredrick

My darling Fredrick

Have you seen him, how tired he is? He works so hard.

I'll go see if he needs anything, he'd like that.

ISABELLA:

"Tell me about them"

He said

"I want to know all about them"

ANNIE: I keep forgetting

I keep forgetting where I am

This is my coat isn't it

It is the right coat

It feels different

ISABELLA: "Tell me" he said.

beat

"Tell me about your wife"

"Tell me about your children"

"Do you see them every day?"

"I don't see my children" he replied "I sent them away"

"Good" I told him "you don't deserve them"

"You're right" he said "I don't"

ANNIE:

It was simple really

From the start I should have known

That day in the snow, she should have been shot

ISABELLA: "He is dead"

"Your Father"

"He was shot"

"He was lined up and shot"

ANNIE: Did you hear?

ISABELLA: Of course

ANNIE: Did you hear what I said?

Pause

ISABELLA: You have to kill me

ANNIE: Or I'll tell everyone

ISABELLA: And be shamed

ANNIE: Humiliated

ISABELLA: Maybe even tried

ANNIE: And killed

ISABELLA: Yes, I heard everything

ANNIE: So, it can't go on

ISABELLA: I know

ANNIE: You leave me with no choice

ISABELLA: I know

ANNIE: She will be shot

Pause

ISABELLA: Yes

ANNIE: Or you will be sent away

ISABELLA: I know

ANNIE: And I will be abandoned

ISABELLA: I see

ANNIE: Is that what you want

ISABELLA: What do you think?

Pause

ISABELLA: I'll do it

ANNIE: What?

ISABELLA: Let me do it myself

ANNIE: But Fredrick...

ISABELLA: It's easier

ANNIE: Yes

ISABELLA: And quicker

ANNIE: Now?

ISABELLA: Yes

ANNIE: How?

ISABELLA: I'll hold it to my head

ANNIE: And shoot

ISABELLA: Yes

ANNIE: And then you'll be free

ISABELLA: Yes

ANNIE: Will you be happy

ISABELLA: When I do it?

ANNIE: When it's done

ISABELLA: Of course, I'll be free.

ANNIE: And you'll come back to

ISABELLA: My Papa

ANNIE: To me.

ISABELLA: I held it there on the side of my head

He turned his back

He didn't want to see

The mess

I'm not sure who would have cleared it up

Maybe no one

It was simple

A shot like Papa.

I did it and dropped the gun

Then I slowly went towards the floor, picked it up and pointed it at him

1, 2, 3,

But

Instead

I just watched

As he crumpled to the floor

And wept

ANNIE: Fredrick

ISABELLA: Fred?

Pause

ANNIE: You fired

ISABELLA: I wanted to do it

ANNIE: I heard you

ISABELLA: It was simple

ANNIE: Just one shot

ISABELLA: I think

ANNIE: Yes

ISABELLA: I can

ANNIE: Fredrick

ISABELLA: With you

ANNIE: My love

ISABELLA: I didn't want to die

ANNIE: It's fine

ISABELLA: I didn't want to die

ANNIE: Enough.

ISABELLA: Don't let me die

Scene 8

ANNIE:

I wore the blue dress again

"Hello my Peacock", he said when he kissed me in the morning

"Tomorrow we'll go riding"

"Not today?" I said.

"No my Darling, remember today is very busy."

"But you look so pretty"

"That will help get me through everything"

ISABELLA:

I slowly un-became myself

Stripped myself of everything I knew

Forgot what I learnt

My life and family disappeared and my mind was filled with lessons of Fred

ANNIE:

It was too icy he said.

The snow had frozen, and it would be like riding on an ice rink

How about ice skating I suggested

What a lovely idea he replied

Let's find a time that suits.

ISABELLA:

There is five minutes when he sits silently in the room looking at the ground

Then slowly he lifts his head and looks at me, and his face softens, his eyes crease as he smiles and he says

"Ah Bella, maybe you will wipe the day from my mind."

ANNIE:

My riding trousers are very old

But can you believe it I still fit into them

He wasn't in his office

And when I rang, no one answered

ISABELLA:

Silence

Only the sound of our breath

1 and 2, 1 and 2

Counting is always so comforting I find, the security in knowing that the next number will automatically land straight into your head, without even trying

Silence

"You're crying", he says

"I'm not", I say

"Why are you crying?"

"I'm not"

"Are you scared?"

"No"

"Then what is it?"

Silence

He walks over to me

And lifts me

He carries me and lies me on the floor

On that cold hard floor, filled with my piss and my sweat and my blood

Where I have slept

Where I have wept

Where he has begged me to love him

But now it's different

He says

"Are you scared"

And I reply

"No"

He leans forward and brushes my hair out of my face and kisses me

"Are you scared now" he says

"No"

And while he holds me I sob, not because it hurts, or it's forced, not because he shouts at me or hits me but because he is soft and tender and gentle. Because he is shaking and when I hold him I feel his whole body tremble and when he holds my face in his hands and looks into my eyes and tells me he loves me I... forget.

ANNIE:

There was a button missing from his coat

A small silver button

The next day it was back

The button was back in its place

ISABELLA:

Do you think I could have the coat back?

ANNIE:

He told me she was dead?

I heard the gun

But there were things that kept changing

A necklace

Gone

His bed never slept in

The way he smelt

ISABELLA:

Oh it's gone

I see

ANNIE:

Could you leave me

Just for a moment

You don't need to watch me

I promise I won't do anything

I just think

I just think

I need to be quite alone

Scene 9

Annie enters the cellar with a bucket of water. The two women stare at each other, unsure who should speak first.

ANNIE: Take your dress off

Take it off!

ISABELLA: –

ANNIE: Do it!

You're practically a child

ISABELLA: –

ANNIE: Turn around

Isabella slowly starts to turn around

ANNIE: What are these marks on your back?

ISABELLA: –

ANNIE: You are beaten?

ISABELLA: No

ANNIE: What are the marks on your back?

ISABELLA: The floor iced over and my skin stuck to it

ANNIE: Why were you on the floor?

ISABELLA: We slept on it, me and my family.

ANNIE: Let me look at them.

Isabella shows her.

Annie lightly touches her back, tracing the outline of her wounds with her finger.

ANNIE: They're so red.

Have you seen them?

Have you seen how red they are?

Are you in pain?

ISABELLA: No

ANNIE: Has Fredrick seen them

ISABELLA: Yes

ANNIE: He has?

What does he think?

Pause

ANNIE: What does he think about the marks on your back?

ISABELLA: He is sorry

ANNIE: Sorry?

ISABELLA: Yes, Fred is sorry.

ANNIE: Fred?

What?

ISABELLA: Fred

ANNIE: Yes, is that what you call him?

ISABELLA: Yes

ANNIE: My Fredrick

ISABELLA: Yes

ANNIE: What does he call you?

Isabella says nothing

Annie jams her finger into Isabella's wounds

ANNIE: What does he call you?

ISABELLA: He calls me Bella

ANNIE: Fred and Bella

You call my husband Fred

Fred

Is that what you say while he is fucking you?

Silence as she begins to clean Isabella

Fredrick and I met at the Ballet, in Berlin and he found me crying.

I could have been a dancer do you know that, maybe we would have danced together.

I could have been anything I wanted to be, a dancer, a doctor, an actress, imagine me in all those films, everyone looking at me.

Look at me

Do you think I'm beautiful?

Do you think I'm beautiful?

ISABELLA: Yes, I think you're very beautiful

ANNIE: I suppose I am,

He asked me if I found the ballet as boring as he did.

Did you hear me? Fred said that. He said he found the ballet boring.

Why dance around a stage when you can dance around a room imagine what people would say if they saw Captain Annhult's daughter wearing her underwear in front of everyone.

So I didn't dance I married

Marry a man who cannot be beaten. Don't waste time on looks or humour or charm or even love make sure he is strong and make sure he will fight, make sure he cannot be beaten.

And what if he doesn't want me Father – what if he wants another?

"Child: we have money; men always want money."

Do you have any money girl?

ISABELLA: No, I have nothing

ANNIE: You do, you have my Fredrick.

Undo my buttons.

ANNIE: Undo the back of my dress girl

Isabella does so

Annie and Isabella are both in standing in their underwear

Can you see me.

Can you see what I am?

You call my husband Fred

You call my husband Fred

You call my husband Fred

ISABELLA: Mama used to sing to us, every night. And when she had finished we would beg her to sing once more. So she would sing again and again and again until we slept and in my dreams the song would always be there. It would only be in the morning when I woke up that it ended. I can't hear her any more. Why don't you sing to your children, I told Fred about my Mama's song and he said he wished you would sing, he said all you do is sit and wait for him, why don't you sing to your children?

ANNIE: Fredrick said that?

ISABELLA: He said you were sad, you had always been sad. When he first saw you, you were crying, he thinks you will cry forever.

Annie goes to slap Isabella but Isabella manages to stop her, they stand there, Isabella holding Annie's arm. There is a moment, then Annie gives in.

ANNIE: He told me we would go riding.

I wore my blue dress for him

Had Hanna pin my hair

Take my clothes

Do you know I love him?

ISABELLA: Yes

ANNIE: So I must make him happy

ISABELLA: Yes

ANNIE: Go to my room

ISABELLA: –

ANNIE: Take the keys, lock the door and wait for him, wait for your Fred

Do you understand?

ISABELLA: Yes

ANNIE: No, do you understand?

I know you see

I know what he really wants

I'm going to dance for him

And then he will love me again.

Pause

I stink – I smell just like you.

Go.

Scene 10

ISABELLA:

There is a siren and then you are beaten out of bed at 3am for Appell. You stand on the Lagerstrasse until all inmates are counted for.

Often people drop dead so guards lose count and start again.

This can take up to four hours, then breakfast and then work.

I have never been to Appell, I have only heard stories.

I arrived in her room at 3am

And I could hear the sirens

So I opened all the windows and stood until Fred arrived.

This was my first Appell.

ANNIE:

First position second position third position.

I have the straightest spine

Look, look at me standing… perfect.

First position second position third position

ISABELLA:

If I had left

Walked out of the door

Through the gates

And onwards

If I had left

This place

Where would I have gone?

To the …

That life

That world

That neither you nor I can picture correctly

Or maybe I'd have been shot

Like Papa

ANNIE:

All I have to do is wait for him

It won't be long

When he sees me, what I have done for him

He will love me like he loves her.

And then we can go back to the ballet. And she can disappear.

ISABELLA:

I can't remember Papa not looking like him

I think of them both with the same eyes and nose and ears and laugh

They are now the same man, identical in my memory

He has trampled all over his face and I can't remember Papa not being like him

But

I do remember the ease in which my father loved me

How simple it was for him

His little girl

His littlest girl

And the ease with which I loved…

With which I love him

ANNIE:

He came for me

And for one small moment

All was well.

ISABELLA:

I fixed the vase after he smashed it

I couldn't find all the pieces

So there were a few gaps

Promise me Papa said

Promise me that you will live.

ISABELLA: Hello

ANNIE: Hello

ISABELLA: No one saw me

ANNIE: No one has seen me

ISABELLA: I don't know what to do

ANNIE: I see now, I see what you wanted.

ISABELLA: She gave me the key

ANNIE: You have the key, you can come and go as you like and I will always be here waiting for you, like her.

ISABELLA: I don't know where to go

ANNIE: Hold me?

ISABELLA: I could have left you. I could have walked out of this house.

ANNIE: I'm different aren't I? But don't be scared, I've changed for you.

ISABELLA: But I would never see you again.

ANNIE: They took all my clothes, after I danced in the snow, they took all my clothes.

ISABELLA: So I came here

ANNIE: And I'll dance at the party

ISABELLA: And waited for you

ANNIE: And then I'll wait for you

ISABELLA: In this room

ANNIE: In this room

ISABELLA: Because…

ANNIE: I love you

ISABELLA: Look at me.

ANNIE: Look at me, look at the marks on my back.

ISABELLA: I'm not her

ANNIE: I'm like her,

ISABELLA: My Fred

ANNIE: It will be our secret.

ISABELLA: We can be together

ANNIE: We will be together again.

ISABELLA: That's what you wanted

ANNIE: That's what you wanted

ISABELLA: And I will dance for you.

ANNIE: And I can dance for you.

ISABELLA: Like the beginning.

ANNIE: Like the beginning.

A moment as both women wait for Fred then slowly Annie begins to realise that Fred may not stay with her.

Remember when we first met Fredrick, and I was crying and you told me to stop. Well look, I'm not crying anymore.

Where are you going?

ISABELLA: Come here

ANNIE: Fredrick look at me, look at me,

ISABELLA: Lock the door Fred. And let's sleep.

ANNIE: Give me the key, what are you doing, no, no, no, no, no, you are meant to love me, you are meant to love me like you used to. Why don't you notice me? I've done this for you. Fred? Fred? I'm crying please, please tell me to stop, I can't stop without you. Remember; remember when we met at the ballet. Please Fred, Fred. Tell me to stop, tell me to stop tell me to stop. Fredrick my Fredrick.

Annie is banging, scratching and screaming at the door, on her knees she slowly curls up into a ball and sobs.

Scene 11

ISABELLA:

She screamed for days

The whole house was filled with her

And we carried on

Like nothing had changed

For the first time in a long time I began to feel human

When you fight for your life

Everything is excusable, don't you think?

ANNIE: Your shoes aren't shined

You need to make sure your shoes are always shined.

Otherwise your uniform doesn't matter

ISABELLA:

It wasn't difficult

ANNIE:

Have you seen?

My arms and legs?

ISABELLA: To forget

ANNIE: Bruised from all the dancing I expect.

ISABELLA: To begin…

ANNIE: Can I have something to eat?

ISABELLA: To begin a life

ANNIE: Some breakfast maybe

ISABELLA: Do you know what a luxury it is to know exactly what is going to happen the following day?

ANNIE: Breakfast is the most important meal of the day

ISABELLA: We'd start the day with breakfast together in our room.

ANNIE: It's Fredrick's favourite meal.

ISABELLA: We read

ANNIE: Fred will read, while she dresses.

ISABELLA: Sometimes we stayed in bed all day.

ANNIE: Fred is always dressed first thing in the morning.

ISABELLA: Yes, he worked; he had to work.

ANNIE: She will walk him to his car.

ISABELLA: Everything was improving.

ANNIE: It's good to support him

ISABELLA: He said

ANNIE: To listen to him

ISABELLA: I had to believe him

ANNIE: She must be a good wife to him

ISABELLA: He came back for lunch

ANNIE: He doesn't come home for lunch

ISABELLA: And we...

ANNIE: Sometimes he doesn't even eat lunch so I send the driver with a bar of chocolate. Yes, we still have chocolate. I hope she knows about the chocolate.

ISABELLA: ...we ate chocolate in bed.

ANNIE: He is very tired when he comes home and often she won't see him. It's the stress of the job you see.

ISABELLA: He changed. His collar used to be tight, smart. But it became loose. I liked him like that, he looked human, he looked just like you, not like a ...

ANNIE: She must learn to love him, the right way. The way I love him.

ISABELLA: I loved him

ANNIE: And he will learn to love me the way he loves her.

ISABELLA: She stayed downstairs

ANNIE: And soon he will notice me.

ISABELLA: She isn't well, he says.

ANNIE: I'll dance for him.

ISABELLA: She has never been well

ANNIE: It's such a happy life

ISABELLA: It was a life

ANNIE: Such a happy life we have

ISABELLA: I never thought I'd have one

ANNIE: I hope she knows

ISABELLA: Mama was right

ANNIE: How to make him happy

ISABELLA: A very long lifeline

ANNIE:

I thought it was Fredrick when you found me

Fred?

Who are you?

Why are you all here?

No one is allowed down here, did my husband say you could come?

Don't touch me

Don't you see?

I'm waiting for him

Let me stay

I'm practising

For the party,

I'm going to dance at a party

There will be music and dancing and Champagne

Lots of Champagne

You'll see me then.

So go, go back to work.

There is lots of work to be done.

Great change is coming, and we are part of it.

I can't leave yet not until he has come

Where is he?

He must watch me dance

You want me to tell you where he is, if I know where he is.

He never came back

After the first time

When he held me in his arms and rocked me back and forth

"What have you done my love, what have you done"

He never came back.

Scene 12

Silence as Isabella and Annie sit and wait for Fred to come to them.

ISABELLA:

He left in the middle of the night.

Just before you arrived

It was as if he knew you were coming.

We had a month together.

In that room, in that beautiful room.

No one knew

If they did, they didn't care.

It's silly to care about a love affair when a war is going on.

Sometimes he would sneak me out and I would sit in the garden

And look at the grass

The colour of the grass

He left in the middle of the night

And said nothing to me

You thought I was her didn't you

But then you found the cellar

And couldn't quite place me.

I don't know where my family are

I suppose everyone has lost their family

And don't pretend you know

That you can find them for me

That they survived

No one survived

Only me

And should I be sorry that I am not among the dead ones?

Because I'm not, I'm not sorry, I'm not sorry that I lived.

ANNIE:

Don't take that away

The photograph

The one of us dancing

I don't care what you do with the rest

Just don't take that away

ISABELLA:

Have you ever been scared to dream?

When you dream, you disappear, you can go home, people who died can talk to you, hold you, love you.

When I dream I fleetingly visit it, my home, my street, Margo, Mama's song, Strudel, Madam Schinifer's Strudel, sofas, cushions, the sound of the front door when it opens. Flowers on the table, grass, the smell of grass, the colour... I can't remember colours. Here everything is grey.

How disappointing to fleetingly visit somewhere then wake up

That's why I can't dream anymore

It's too disappointing.

ANNIE:

I think I'd like to go now?

Is that allowed?

Can you ask someone to organise a car?

Because

I think I'd like to go

Back to Berlin

To our beautiful house

ISABELLA:

I suppose I'm free

You know I don't know where he is

So I'm useless to you

beat

I feel that when I walk out of this house everything will be silent

And that it'll take no time at all to go back

That I'll just arrive

That I'll think of home and there I'll be

So perfectly simple

I feel that when I walk out of this house everything will be silent

ANNIE:

Do you think you could

Give this to them

My children

Could you give them this photograph of us

Of Fredrick and I

So they know

ISABELLA:

I'll eat strudel with Margo

ANNIE:

When his job began

ISABELLA:

And I'll hold Mama,

ANNIE:

And we moved

ISABELLA:

And when it gets cold we will leap around the room

ANNIE:

To this house

ISABELLA:

1 and 2 and 3 and 4

ANNIE:

They caught a girl trying to escape.

Through a hole, in the fence

Fredrick was called

And

He made them all stand in the Lagerstrasse

The girl was brought forward

And Fredrick…

He stripped her

He placed his gun on the back of her head

And counted

1, 2, 3

He moved the gun away

And then on four he hit her with it

On five he hit her head

On six her stomach

On seven her chest and on and on and on 8, 9, 10, 11, 12

He beat her

He beat her to death

Then he came home

Woke me up

And asked me to run him a bath

And as I bathed him, as I wiped the blood of the girl off his arms, as I washed the blood of the girl out of his hair, as I held his hand and kissed his fingers, he told me everything, piece by piece, number by number. When it was over we slept, he held me all night and in the morning when we woke he said to me

"How about a party?"

"A party? Of course my love."

"With music" he said "and dancing and champagne lots of champagne."

Scene 13

The two women, for perhaps the last time, find themselves face to face.

ANNIE: They found my coat.

ISABELLA: Good

ANNIE: I lost it.

ISABELLA: I'm glad you have it back.

ANNIE: He gave me this

ISABELLA: I know

ANNIE: Did you wear it

Pause

ISABELLA: Yes, yes I did, I'm sorry

ANNIE: It's alright

ISABELLA: What did you tell them?

ANNIE: A story

ISABELLA: What story

ANNIE: The story of Fredrick and I

ISABELLA: He left

ANNIE: I know

ISABELLA: Did he come to you?

ANNIE: When?

ISABELLA: Before he left?

ANNIE: No

ISABELLA: Did he see you dance?

ANNIE: No

ISABELLA: I'm sorry

ANNIE: Why?

ISABELLA: I'm sorry he didn't see you dance

ANNIE: It doesn't matter

ISABELLA: Where will you go?

ANNIE: To the ballet

ISABELLA: Which one?

ANNIE: Giselle, it's my favourite

ISABELLA: Yes,

ANNIE: I'll wear my coat

ISABELLA: Yes?

ANNIE: And my dress with the gold buttons

ISABELLA: You'll look beautiful

ANNIE: Do you think I'm beautiful

ISABELLA: Yes, very much so

Silence

Isabella goes to leave

ANNIE: We have farms in Munich

Isabella stops

ANNIE: He loved it there, maybe he is visiting, getting the horses ready for a ride. If he isn't there when you arrive, don't leave, he will probably have fallen asleep by the lake, so just wait for him. The stables are warm, you can wait there, he will find you I'm sure, and maybe you can go riding together. Will you let me know, if you come back, if you went riding? I do so love to ride. And if he asks if I'm alright, if he asks if I'm well, tell him I'm fine, tell him I'm wonderful. Tell him I'm. Dancing...